MEEK

Inspirational Poetry of a Humble Servant

J. Thomas Maultsby, Jr.

Dayton, Ohio

Written by J. Thomas Maultsby, Jr.

OPOL Publishing Staff:

Executive Editor, Patricia Hastings, Esq.
Assistant Editor, Charity Scott, Presidential Scholar in Journalism, University of
        Alabama Class of 2008.
Owner/Publisher, J. Thomas Maultsby, Jr.
        OPOLPublishing.com
        P.O. Box 60009
        Dayton, OH 45406
        937-367-6985

A Special Thanks to Terry Anderson, graphic designer and publishing consultant, who was instrumental in bringing this project to fruition.

Printed by Bookmasters, Inc., Ashland, Ohio

Web orders: http://www.atlasbooks.com/marktplc/02515.htm
E-mail orders: orders@bookmasters.com
Phone orders: 800-247-6553
Fax orders: 419-281-6883

ISBN: 9780615230030

MEEK

Inspirational Poetry of a Humble Servant

Acknowledgements

I am indebted to so many people who have had a significant impact on my life and the writing of this book.

My loving wife, Frances, who supports everything I do; James T. Maultsby, Sr. and Dorothy M. Maultsby, Esquire (deceased), my parents, who, having migrated to Washington, D.C. from Whiteville, North Carolina, raised me in the way I should go; my older sister and best friend ever, Wanda Jane Maultsby, who only lived until age 23; James Daniel Debeuneure, my first cousin, who was a big brother to me, and was murdered on September 11, 2001, in the plane that was deliberately flown into the Pentagon by terrorists; my younger sister Myra Maultsby, whom I love very much; and my son Thomas III, with whom I especially enjoyed playing basketball as he was learning to be a man.

Savannah Gibson and Thelma Osborne, two of my mom's life-long best friends were always lovingly there for my sisters and me in the good times, but especially in the challenging times as we were growing up; and all the neighbors on the 200 block of Oneida St. NE Washington, DC.

Mentioned here are some of the people who played a major role in my spiritual development over the years: all of the people at John Wesley AMEZ Church in Washington, D.C., where I grew up; Reverend Charles Larkin Scott, Sr., who taught me how to have a meaningful relationship with Jesus Christ; Pastor Arthur L. McGuire, Joshua Christian Ministries in Dayton, Ohio, who is a dear friend and spiritual advisor; Mickey Reeves and Joseph Taylor, who are my Sunday school leaders at Greater Allen AME Church in Dayton, Ohio; Frances Taylor (deceased), my play mom in Dayton, Ohio, who nurtured, guided and prayed fervent prayers for me daily; and Phyllis Caldwell and Lottie Rivers, two saints in my church who motivated me and prayed for me throughout this entire project.

Finally, our only grandchild, Jakub Michael Mudd who is a blessing out of the union of our wonderful son-in-law Jason Michael Mudd and our beautiful daughter Kendra Maultsby Mudd. Jakub was born May 8, 2008, and has provided me with the renewed joy and exhilaration that I experienced when our kids were born. He is grandpa's new best friend.

MEEK

Inspirational Poetry of a Humble Servant

Blessed are the Meek for they will inherit the earth.
(Matthew 5:5)

Meek is showing patience and humility;
gentle; humble in spirit or manner.

MEEK

Only two men were ever called meek in the scriptures--Moses and Jesus. They were strong, but their lives were yielded to God. Their strength was under control. When Moses faced the Pharaoh and when Jesus faced the Pharisees, they were still obedient to God's reins (Moses: KJV Numbers 12:3; Jesus: KJV 2 Corinthians 10:1).

Meekness is a virtue in the kingdom of heaven (Matt 5:5). It is part of Christ likeness that is produced in us by his Spirit (Gal 5:23). It should be our constant attitude as we represent God's kingdom to outsiders (1 Pet 3:15).

Remember that meekness does not grow out of weakness, but from power held under control.

Table of Contents

About The Author   i-ii

Meek   1

A Walk By Faith   3

A Mother's Love   7

Catastrophe In America   11

Christian Man   15

Christmas In America   19

Congrats!   23

God's Giving   27

Death   29

Easter   33

Forgive   37

God Does Not Discriminate   41

Godly Friends   45

Jesus' Church   49

Marriage   55

Nothing To Do With Living   59

Obesity   63

Religion   67

Remember Me   71

Sin   75

Thanksgiving   79

The Passing   83

Thug Life   85

About the Author

J. Thomas Maultsby, Jr.

Writing this book was a two year journey of reflection and contemplation about things that impacted my life. It was a period of intense spiritual introspection; an examination that touched every emotion, feeling and thought about the poems that were born from this experience. The composition of these poems emanated from a compelling desire to express the inspiration that drove my passion for speaking power to truth. It was an indwelling spirit for that period, which could not be contained.

There were many situations and circumstances that came into the path of my life that prompted these writings. For example, the poem Walk by Faith was written following the sudden and unexpected illness of the spouse of a business colleague for whom I have enormous respect. A Mother's Love was written to acknowledge an unselfish expression of love and prayer that I constantly received from a very dear woman who was my wife's best friend's mother and she had enough love for anyone who came into her life. Obesity was written out of my passion to fight this problem that spawns so maney diseases of anyone who becomes a victim of its awesome grip.

The primary motivation for all these works was my passion for Jesus Christ. Once my heart was touched by each subject and following fervent prayer, the words came effortlessly, so it seemed, at the time. The reason the book took two years is because I did not know that I was writing a book until I composed the twentieth poem. I felt that I was simply pacifying my desire for spiritual expression.

While I remain somewhat intrigued about why I was moved to produce these works, I have benefited tremendously from the experience and hope those of you who read the poems will benefit as well.

J. Thomas Maultsby, Jr. is a native Washington DC and graduate of Calvin Coolidge High School. He left DC to attend Wilberforce University where he earned BS Degree in Business Management. He was then awarded an ASPO-Ford Foundation Fellowship at the University of Cincinnati and completed a two year masters program in Community Planning with a collateral field of study in Organizational Development. Thomas is a life member of Wilberforce University and the University of Cincinnati alumni associations and Kappa Alpha Psi Fraternity.

Thomas held many leadership and executive professional positions with private and public sector companies such as, American Management Association, DDI, Price Waterhouse, Unity Bank, Seven Hills Neighborhood Houses, Montgomery County Community Action and United Way of Dayton. He has also managed a small business incubator and served as an administrator in higher education and instructor for the Ohio Certified Public Manager Program.

Thomas is owner and Group Leader of Group One Development, LLC (www. G1D.us) a professional service consulting and training company that has worked with fortune companies, government and nonprofit organizations for twenty one years.

Thomas is also owner and publisher of OPOL Publishing started in 2004. A company formed to help combat illiteracy and improve reading skills of all people. OPOL specializes in writing and publishing works that are about one hundred pages or less. Reading an entire book can be a major incentive for improving reading skill and we intend to provide many such opportunities with our publication.

He also formed Christian Sabbath Fellowship (CSF) which is an organization that helps people to establish a loving relationship with God. CSF also gives to those in need. He and his wife are members of Greater Allen A.M.E. Church in Dayton, Ohio.

Thomas has served on over 30 boards and commissions throughout his career and chaired a third of them. He currently serves as the chairperson of the board of a very large Ohio based health care management company and its community-based foundation.

Thomas and Frances Maultsby have been married for 32 years; they have two children; Kendra Maultsby Mudd and Tommy Maultsby, III who now live in Durham, North Carolina. His baby sister Myra L. Maultsby, an independent consultant, still resides in their hometown of Washington, DC.

MEEK

Meek

Meek is strength which is antithetical
to what many believe to be weak,
Meek is humility, self-control and tranquility;
qualities that Gods' people seek.

Meek is power that is spiritually reflected
in the makeup of ones facade,
Meek is the way that we humbly
submit to praise and honor God.

The bible espouses, the meek
are the ones who will inherit the earth,
Meek is the one, who delivered that promise
after an immaculate birth.

The meek will enjoy spiritual satisfaction
by obeying Gods' instructions,
But one who sows with a sinful nature
will ultimately reap destruction.

The meek will sow with a spirit of salvation
because they strive to do what is right,
Their humble demeanor can be deceiving
while their spirit embodies the light.

Meek are those who cling to hope
and gain wisdom from life lessons learned,
Meek are the ones, who will surely meet Jesus
on the day that he returns.

Meek is the spirit that consumed the author
as these words were put into print,
Meek is the way that he hopes you're inspired
to discern the books' godly intent.

✝✝✝

**When faced with a malady or illness
faith will assure your ultimate well-being.**

*O Lord my God, I called to you
for help and you healed me.*

Psalm 30:2

A Walk By Faith

One day you're up and walking
and the next you're on your back.
It appears somewhat ironic,
although it is a fact.

When affliction is upon you,
it's common to say "Why me."
In these times one might wonder,
what God would have you see.

Now faith is but a concept
until it is applied.
The acceptance of its power
will keep one's hope alive,

We live in the present moment,
at least so it seems,
Tomorrow is not promised
and yesterday's a dream.

Affliction's a temporary setback
for one who walks by faith,
Now God will send a blessing
and He's never, ever late.

Loved ones will remain in prayer mode
as you recuperate,
So hold your head up to the sky,
and keep it good and straight,

Every time you read this prayer
your faith will be revived,
Praise the Lord and count your blessings;
you're very much alive.

The healing power in this message
for you is now proclaimed,
So walk by faith and not by sight
and you will never be the same.

Accept this as a fervent prayer for you,
in Jesus' Holy Name.

FAITH

**The love of a mother is second
only to that of the Lord.**

*May your father and mother be glad;
may she who gave you birth rejoice.*

Proverbs 23:25

A Mother's Love

Honor your mother
and your father too,
Are words of wisdom
that God gives to you,.

A mother's love reaches
far and wide,
Within her tender touch
you can always abide.

She is made to nurture,
care and forgive,
To raise you in a way
that God would have you live.

A mother's love is permanent;
it doesn't go away,
For better or worse,
she loves you come what may.

Even when a mother
has trials and tribulations,
Her love is unconditional,
without any reservations.

God made mothers special
to give the gift of life,
Remember, it's your duty
to always treat her nice.

A mother's love is special,
so keep her in your heart,
And from this very special love
you will not depart.

A mother's love is special,
love her everyday,
May her love forever bless you,
In Jesus' Name we pray.

LOVE

**God is there in good times and bad,
we just need the will to believe
and the desire to want Him.**

*God is our refuge and strength,
an ever-present help in trouble.
Therefore we will not fear,
though the earth give way
and the mountains fall into the
heart of the sea, though its waters
roar and foam and the mountains
quake with their surging.*

Psalms 46:1-3

Catastrophe
In America

The world is experiencing catastrophes
that take a lot of lives,
With advanced technology in telecom
we can see them with our eyes.

Tornadoes, hurricanes, tsunami, earthquakes,
fires, floods and terrorist attacks,
It makes your nerves stand on edge,
and you wonder who really has your back.

The times of tribulation are prophesized
in the book of Revelations,
Yet we all seem very astonished
at what is happening throughout the nations.

God made the world and all its inhabitants,
no matter where they live,
In such times, we should help each other
and yes, we should give.

One may ask where God is
when these things come about,
We pray to him our shallow prayers
with trepidation, worry and doubt.

Without such problems we commit
our sins and move God out of the way,
Why should we have the expectation
that He will save the day?

I truly believe the world does not function
the way that God intended,
My greatest fear is that we hurt Him so bad
that he may decide today to end it.

But while we are here we must be resilient,
recover, and live His way,
Express our sorrow, rebuild our nation
and continue to learn how to pray.

I really believe when things happen
there is a divine purpose in mind,
I pray dear lord no matter how I die,
I don't get left behind.

Catastrophe in America
is a traumatic experience for anyone involved,
Some things are just beyond our control
which we can not solve.

Some how I still love this country
because in the end it belongs to God,
So with the next catastrophe we experience,
like Moses I'll raise my rod.

That does not mean a mountain will move
or that the sea will part,
It means, pray fervent prayers
and keep God first in your heart.

AMERICA

**Christian men must understand
the importance of their duties
and act accordingly.**

*You, man of God,
pursue righteousness, godliness,
faith, love and gentleness.*

1 Timothy 6:11

Christian Man

A man of God must face reality
and step up to the plate,
The elements of his life must not be subject
to an ungodly fate.

He must lead his family with courage
to know and love the Lord,
He must exemplify the role model
that his children will adore.

A Christian man is forward
in his godly presentation,
His walk is never ending
in his spiritual gestation.

The character of a Christian man
reflects all of God's Laws,
He can never submit to the sin filled world
no matter how much it calls.

A Christian man will confess his sins,
and keep a clear and focused mind,
He will never run the race of life
where he gets left behind.

A Christian man is saved, sanctified,
holy and studies only the truth,
He understands his primal nature
and the essence of his roots.

He looks upon abdication of duty
with impatience and disdain,
He knows to walk the straight and narrow
means a lot more of the same.

You see a Christian man leads a simple life;
he seeks the ultimate prize,
If you are not this way, to make a change,
would render you very wise.

A Christian man will serve the Lord,
the church and, yes his wife,
A Christian man has but one goal,
to seek eternal life.

A Christian man is not a guy
that you will meet every day,
But when you meet him on the street,
you will know it right away.

In case you're not a Christian man,
we have one thing to say,
You can come to Christ today
and be well on your way.

A man is just a partial man
until he turns to Christ,
We hope you get this message
because we have said it more than twice.

This poem is written for every man
who values godly advice,
Don't leave your manhood be determined
by the role of pagan dice.

To be a man, a godly man,
is the reason you were born,
Assume your duties as a faithful servant,
to which God will adorn.

Being a Christian man is your final legacy
when you get called to rest,
The Lord will say,
Well done my good and faithful servant,
you have done your best."

MANKIND

**Jesus' birthday is one of the most
revered religious celebrations in America
and its meaning is diminishing.**

*Today in the town of David
a Savior has been born to you;
He is Christ the Lord.*

Luke 2:11

Christmas In America

The sanctity of Christmas in America
is starting to be a joke,
Every time it's challenged
many of our leaders seem to choke.

In countries that you travel to
whose culture is very strong,
Recognize a primary religion
to which its citizens belong.

When foreigners take up residence
other countries do not fold,
Their stance upon their values
is upright, strong and bold.

Some want to call Christmas in America
just another holiday,
Because it's deemed politically incorrect
to celebrate Jesus' birthday.

We took God out of public schools
without much of a fuss,
I wonder what the Founders meant
by the phrase "In God We Trust".

The Ten Commandments cannot be displayed
in the court house halls,
The irony is that they seem to be
the basis for our country's laws.

Christmas in America
is not what it used to be,
Some would even change the name
of the Christmas tree.

Santa Claus, Jingle Bells
all seem to be okay,
But they really don't symbolize
the Christmas holiday.

Jesus is the only reason
for the Christmas season,
To abandon that fact in the USA
would be pretty close to treason.

So let's collect our thoughts, recapitulate
and focus on the truth,
We have to do the righteous thing
to preserve our Christian roots.

Christmas is just as American
as barbeque and apple pie,
There is no way a God fearing citizen
would let its culture die.

Take a stand for Christmas
and be grateful for His birth,
This is what makes America
the greatest country on Earth.

Christmas in America is
not what it used to be,
But it has not lost its meaning for Christians
like you and me.

So when you hear detractors
and those who want to hate,
Just turn the other cheek
and continue to celebrate.

When you sing Christmas songs
and you carol door to door,
And raise a ten foot Christmas tree
in the middle of your floor,

Remember, Christmas in America
is not what it used to be,
Thank God for Jesus Christ
who still lives inside of me.

Christmas in America
is not what it used to be,
The power in the birth of Jesus Christ
is the reason why we're free,

Christmas in America
will never go astray,
If we continue to celebrate
until Jesus returns one day,

Although Christmas in America
is not what it used to be,
Christmas in America
still means the same to me.

**Children must be encouraged
to be their best in all they do.**

*Even a child is known by his action,
by whether his conduct is pure and right.*

Proverbs 20:11

Congrats!

Congratulations students
on your academic prowess,
You've achieved great success
as God would allow it.

As you advance in life remember
that learning never stops
It requires a lifetime commitment
if you plan to reach the top.

Learning is more than studying
and the books that you may read,
It's the foundation for success
if you plant the proper seeds.

Learning is a process
that can elevate your mind,
It's a line of demarcation
between failure and the sublime.

Knowledge is important,
and you must be well read,
But knowledge has no power
lying dormant in your head.

Apply your gifts and talents
to help each other out,
Practice forgiveness, love, mercy,
not hate, violence and doubt.

Your mind must always focus
on the good that you can do,
It is easy to be negative,
if that is what you choose.

I just came to tell you
that faith without works is dead,
I hope this simple message
is registering in your head.

Being smart is quite alright
if that is who you are,
Knowledge plus wisdom
is power and can take you very far.

I have given you the formula
to continue your success,
Adhere to this mighty truth
so that you can do your best.

Accept your honors with great humility
don't get intoxicated with pride,
And remember to share your gifts
with others as you travel far and wide.

Congrats! is what I tell you
as this poem comes to a close.

If you encounter setbacks
and forget where you are going,
Just read this poem, thank the Lord
and reclaim victory in the morning.

CELEBRATE

**Giving is a blessing
for the giver and the receiver.**

*Give and it will be given to you.
A good measure, pressed down,
shaken together and running over,
will be poured into your lap.
For with the measure you use,
it will be measured to you.*

Luke 6:38

God's Giving

You can't beat God's giving no matter what you do,
His giving is a testimony to His mighty love for you

You can't beat Gods giving no matter how you try,
Even if you think you can, you simply live a lie.

God is very generous with the portion He lets you keep,
You get 90, He gets 10 so the tithe seems rather cheap.

God so loves the world he gave His only Son,
I feel somewhat ashamed that I get 9, and He gets 1.

I think tithing is a test to see what we will do,
Will you glorify the Lord with the 90 He gives to you?

God so love the world that He gave it all to us,
He gave us great dominion with agape love and trust.

10 just seems to be so little for such generosity,
So, I'm going to try to give him as much as he gives me.

To prove your endless love for him, you must even the score,
You have to flip the script on tithing, and give a whole lot more.

With faith the size of a mustard seed your 10 will multiply,
Take advice from a humble servant and give largely until you die.

**Death is but a transition
and new beginning for the believer.**

*That everyone who believes in him
may have eternal life.*

John 3:15

Death Poem

Death could be the end of your life
or the beginning of something new,
The body turns to dust, the spirit returns
to God after leaving you.

It is the valor of a Christian
to accept the rewards of a physical death,
For it is with faith and not fear
that one endures their final earthly breath.

You can die and still be living
 if you choose a life of sin,
Or you can make a conscience decision
to be born again.

You see, death is ever present,
no matter who you are,
It hovers above your being
as if it were a star.

Death is a gateway to eternal life
for the Christian believer,
But the sting of death has a different fate
when you submit to the deceiver.

Dying in the name of Jesus
will negate sins retribution,
Your spirit will rest with God All Mighty
and avoid hell's dissolution.

Dying is a state of sleep
that every believer will face,
It will culminate the eternal power
of God's all mighty grace.

So when you see a Christian die,
rejoice and do not be sad,
Death brings about God's judgment
for those both good and bad.

Maybe the death of one you love
is a calling card for you,
Claim Jesus Christ as Lord and Savior
and live forever too.

One thing that we know for sure
is that all the living will face death,
Confess your sins and make peace with God
so that you will forever rest.

It is Jesus desire to receive your spirit
when your final days are done,
When you have run your best race
and kept God number one.

Die in peace with the guarantee
that you are God's son or daughter,
Inherit your gift of eternal life
and claim your heavenly quarters.

Death is just the beginning of life
when God's word you have obeyed,
Be thankful for the narrow path you walk
and that you have not strayed.

Death is a circumstance,
from which you cannot run,
But with God's grace and mercy
it can be overcome.

UPLIFT

**Easter symbolizes the completion of salvation,
the greatest gift of love given to sinners.**

*He saved us, not because of righteous things
we had done, but because of his mercy.
He saved us through the washing
of rebirth and renewal by the holy spirit.*

Titus 3:5

Easter

Sorry little children
if this poem is a little disappointing,
But the Easter bunny's legacy
is void of the anointing.

Parents we must emphasize
the power of the resurrection story,
So that our children will praise the Lord
with the right outlook on Glory.

On Friday He was crucified,
on the Sabbath He laid at rest,
And on Sunday He arose
again to be His very best.

He spent another forty days
to certify His mission,
He then ascended into heaven
in hopes of our submission.

The Easter bunny is okay
 because God loves animals too,
But we must keep the bunny in perspective
because he can't save me or you.

As we wear our pretty clothes
and hunt for Easter eggs,
Thank Jesus Christ in your prayers
before you go to bed.

Easter is a happy time
for it comes in early spring,
What a time for life's renewal
as butterflies spawn their wings.

What we must keep in mind
as we as feast and celebrate,
Jesus is an awesome Lord;
He's magnificent, and He is great.

Jesus died and rose again
so that we can live forever
He's a living God who dwells within,
whose love we cannot sever.

It's the burden of sin that God
lifted as he sacrificed His Son,
No one else could save the world
the way that He has done.

As we gather today to praise the Lord
for His redemption, which gives us life,
We must humble ourselves to His love
and mercy and forever be contrite.

The resurrection of Jesus, in the life if a Christian,
is a most holy holiday,
Let's fold our hands and bow our heads
as we begin to pray.

Dear Lord we bless, honor and cherish you,
and thank you for your Son,
And every time we think of Easter
we'll know that He's the one.

Easter bonnets and brand new suits,
today we may adorn,
But never forget the resurrection,
and the reason Jesus was born.

Praise the Lord on the holiest day,
and your spirits He will lift,
Let's be redeemed and accept salvation
as God's Easter gift, Amen.

RISE

Forgiveness is better for the forgiver than for the forgiven.

Forgive and you will be forgiven.

Luke 6:37

Forgive

Do unto others as you would have them do unto you,
is the essence of the golden rule,
However, doing unto others as they do unto you,
could lead one to be mean and cruel.

Forgiveness requires that you forgive and forget
what another person has done to you,
Not forgiving others means that you can't be forgiven,
for the wrong things that you do.

Why bear the burdens of not forgiving others
and depriving yourself of God's grace,
The Lord will relieve your burdens; honor your obedience
so that you don't lose face.

Forgiveness is an act between people
that epitomizes their love for each other,
It may challenge your will, your need to be still
as your patience is subject to sputter.

Not forgiving is unhealthy, mentally taxing
and triggers unwarranted stress,
Forgiving is healthy and reversing these symptoms
can relieve you from its duress.

If one grows weary in their forgiveness for others,
where should one draw the line?
According to the bible, never grow weary,
you must forgive one seventy-seven times.

Forgiveness is the concept, to which one refers
in the phrase; it's not about me,
To put others first defies our worldly logic
and such selflessness you rarely ever see.

Forgiveness is a gift, given to us by God
to encourage human reconciliation,
When there is a dispute that you can not solve;
let forgiveness be your determination.

Forgive and forget from the depths of one's heart
can change the way people interact,
It would go a long way toward relieving bad feelings
and keeping relationships in tact.

I can not speak for others because I do not know
their druthers, but I will always forgive,
Seventy-seven times is a lot of forgiveness
and it should last as long as I live.

With the power of the Holy Spirit and the love
of God, forgiveness is always abound,
Thank you Jesus for forgiveness, so that relationships
are deeply rooted in godly grounds.

FORGIVE

God is always fair in His Judgment.

The works of his hands are faithful and just.

Psalms 111:7

God Does Not Discriminate

The sun comes up
and it is never late,
Rain falls on everyone,
there is no escape.
God's love is merciful
and he does not discriminate,

Salvation is a gift from God
that can seal a sinner's fate,
His healing power can sooth
any pains or aches.
It is God's nature to love you
and he does not discriminate.

When you are down on yourself
and can't see very straight,
When you feel all alone,
hurt and full of hate.
God knows your suffering, hears your prayer
and he does not discriminate.

God made us all look different
some with curly hair and some with straight,
We are even different sizes
as evidenced by our height and weight.
God appreciates diversity,
but he does not discriminate.

God's nature is in you,
it's divine, and it's innate,
He resides in your spirit;
He is there for goodness sake.
God is your source of power
and he does not discriminate.

God gives us free will
so that we capitulate,
He knows your doubt can lead to sin
and cause you to separate.
God understands your weakness
and he does not discriminate.

We do not know the hour,
the time or place,
So seek him at this moment
and do not hesitate.
Jesus will return to claim the saved
whether they are sleep or awake.

On judgment day
the Lord will come,
for all who patiently wait.
He will read your account
and tally your score
as you hope to elevate,.

One thing is certain
when judgment comes
and God gives you a date.
You can rest assure
that wherever you go
He did not discriminate.

COMPASSION

**True friends do not have to be asked,
they instinctively know when to act
and they expect no payment.**

*Let us not become weary in doing good,
for at the proper time we will reap
a harvest if we do not give up.*

Galatians 6:9

Godly Friends

When in a sticky situation,
a good friend you can expect,
To show up without judging you
as they are circumspect.

You can call them in the morning
or the middle of the night,
They will respond to your call
with great pleasure and delight.

They understand service
as demonstrated by Jesus Christ,
They have no problems with making
an unselfish sacrifice.

A true friend has no limits
to the godly work they do,
They consider their work and service
as a witness to you.

A friend is very perceptive
as she knows just what you need.
She can even mend a broken heart
before it starts to bleed.

A real good friend is caring
whenever your are there,
When you come over to watch the game
he gives you the recliner chair.

A friend is very humble
and will never put you down,
They can help you don a pleasant smile
where there was once a frown.

Friendship is reciprocal
and should always work both ways,
It is embedded in forgiveness
in case one of you strays.

When you're a friend forever,
within you there is a truth,
A power derived from the spirit of God
that will not turn you loose.

Friendship is important because
we never walk alone,
In Jesus you will have a friend
until he calls you home.

FRIENDSHIP

Jesus has but one church in his name and one of its purposes is to unite Christians to spread the gospel.

God household is the church of the living God, the pillar and foundation of the truth.

1 Timothy 3:15

Jesus' Church

Jesus said a body of believers
was the foundation for His church,
He established the mantra for this movement
before he left the earth.

He said, "I build my church
upon this rock which I love as my bride,
And through my church the gospel
will be preached near, far and wide."

Jesus' church had no denominations,
rituals or four cornered walls,
He preached from shores, streets, mountains and boats;
He told the truth to all.

It was Jesus' intent to keep church simple
and save those who live in sin,
His church is one that loves God's people
and invites them all to attend.

Jesus' church would be no mystery,
and it would certainly bear His name,
Jesus Christ would be the reference as
He would have it simple and plain.

In Jesus church there are no reserved seats
for those who come every week,
For in His church all of the seats
are for the poor, humble and meek.

If Jesus' church was still around
what a pleasure it would be to belong,
Hearing the word and doing what is says;
one could never go wrong.

In Jesus church all the members are equal
and treated one in the same,
They gather together to read the scripture,
sing and praise His holy name.

Jesus' church would be open 24/7
and the doors would never be locked,
It would be a refuge for the weary,
hungry and the members of His flock.

Jesus' church would be a storehouse
for goods and services alike,
It would share His bounty with those in need
from daybreak through the night.

I will be glad when Jesus returns
to reclaim His church again,
Perhaps then all God's people
will lament with shame and chagrin.

But if we were wise we would get it together
before that wonderful day,
So then, "Well done my good and faithful servant,"
is all that Jesus would say.

Deep in my soul I am not quite sure
if we operate His church as intended,
So when He returns we should probably expect
that He will abruptly end it.

Between now and then we should put our faith
in the Church of Jesus Christ,
We will bring believers together to praise the Lord
for His ultimate sacrifice.

Jesus' church gives honor to God
and praises Him so that He feels good,
I pray a fervent prayer that Jesus' church
will come to my neighborhood.

One thing is certain as I pray
to my God through Jesus, His only son,
Where two or more are gathered in His holy name
is the church that I am from.

Jesus' church is a body of believers,
who love Him and pledge to do his will,
This is the church, in which I am a member
and will remain until I am still.

In Jesus' church, He is clearly the head
and Him no one can replace,
When you join His church you are well endowed
with His love, mercy and grace.

Jesus' church will go out into the world
to reclaim every woman and man,
But if the world enters the church
because we are not at our post,
the rock becomes sinking sand.

So, the next time you gather in Jesus' holy name
wherever that may be,
That is the church which Jesus established
for believers like you and me.

In Jesus name we pray, Amen.

PRAISE

**Marriage is a religious union
between and man and woman
established by God.**

*For this reason a man will leave
his father and mother and
be united to his wife,
and the two will become one flesh.*

Ephesians 5:31

Marriage as God Intended

Marriage is a spiritual bond
between a woman and a man,
Its Gods divine foundation
for a family plan.

Marriage is more than commitment
when woman and man are one,
You spend a life together
once your vows are done.

Marriage perpetuates life from
the offspring that are sprung,
Raise them up in the way they should go
and from it they won't run.

Sometimes marriage ends in divorce
because the vows are broken,
Maybe within that family's plan
God's word was not spoken.

Children are always hurt
when parents decide to depart,
It rattles their life, rocks their world
and reeks havoc within their hearts.

Marriage should be a partnership
that meets life's ups and downs,
True love should be the virtue
that turns all challenges around.

Jesus was married to his church,
to which he gave his all,
He demonstrated a three year ministry
in a marriage that would not fall.

Perhaps we should take more seriously
what marriage is meant to be,
A man and woman in a life time commitment
of love, faith and unity.

Marriage should not be a trial for sex
or satisfying lustful passion,
It should not be for selfish reasons
of personal satisfaction.

Marriage is a holy bond between
a woman and man,
It is the way that God intended
to populate his land.

So when you take your vows, say I do
and exchange wedding rings,
You would be very wise
to know a couple of things.

What God brings together
for his pleasure should be left intact,
It is our prayer for your marriage
that you at least know that.

But in the event you need more proof
about what marriage means,
Keep God in it in all you do
even in your thoughts and dreams.

Marriage is between and man and a woman
to perpetuate God's plan,
Center you marriage on the love of God
and do the best you can

You will be blessed in all you do
as you remain as one,
You will beat the odds and be an example
in marriage; then you will have won.

MARRIAGE

**Christians must make wise choices
to experience the power of God**

*Repent, then, and return to God,
so that times of refreshing
may come from the Lord.*

Acts 3:19

Nothing to do With Living

There seems to be confusion about the
relevance of the Ten Commandments,
But God did not make a mistake about
the laws in which he granted.

Jesus came to fulfill the law without
fail or to make excuses,
To abdicate his duty would be sin,
for which God has no uses.

Why do people do so many things that
have nothing to do with living?
Instead of obeying the word and accepting
the life that you were given.

Smoking, alcohol and illicit drugs are
all harmful to our health,
Ironically, we do these things as we work
to create more wealth.

We ingest the toxins and chemicals
that are added to processed food,
When enlightened ones try to warn us,
we label them intrusive and rude.

Why do people do so many things
that have nothing to do with living?
Instead of obeying the word
and accepting the life that you were given.

In our impatience, rage and anger
we engage in acts of senseless violence,
In such emotionally charged acts innocent
people can be wrongly silenced.

Polluted air clogs our lungs and
carcinogens line our rivers and streams,
We abuse and misuse these essential
resources by failing to keep them clean.

Why do people do so many things
that have nothing to do with living?
Instead of obeying the word
and accepting the life that you were given.

Is it because we are so selfish
that we live primarily for personal gain?
We emit gases like sulfur dioxide
and nitrogen oxides that make acid rain.

We deprive ourselves of required sleep
which contributes to bad stress,
We operate our bodies in overdrive
in our quest to possess the best.

Why do people do so many things
that have nothing to do with living?
Instead of obeying the word
and accepting the life that you were given.

God created the world
and gave us dominion to rule it with faith and love,
We are to care for His creation
with appreciation for creatures like lions and doves.

Things that have nothing to do with living
are things that we should change,
These are things that make life perplexing
because they are hard to rearrange.

Obeying the word and accepting the life
that Jesus would have you to live,
Will yield the opportunity for you to be blessed,
with all that God has to give.

LIVE

We only get one body and we should keep it healthy and pure for the Lord.

Do you not know that your body is a temple of the Holy Spirit, who is in you, whom you have received from God? You are not your own;

1 Corinthians 6:19

Obesity

Obesity is a monster
that can overtake your life,
It creates ill health, enslavement,
stress and cellular strife.

It can transform your body
in a short amount of time,
It has no mercy, makes no excuses;
it just manipulates your mind.

You look into a mirror
and know exactly what you see,
Yet your eating habits continue
and you say, "I'm just a bigger me".

Obesity is a killer,
it even eats your self esteem,
thoughts of being smaller
seem to be an impossible dream.

"Accept me as I am"
becomes your defensive cry,
Yet deep inside your soul
you know you live a lie.

If you ever want to lose
the dangerous weight you've gained,
You must understand the solution
is lodged within your brain.

Diets do not work;
they offer temporary relief,
To reverse the grip of obesity
you must change your core beliefs.

Unlike a bad hair day,
you can not hide it with a hat,
You can not reduce it
by wearing something black.

Obesity is created by sedentary living,
empty calories and saturated fat,
In order to overcome it
you must have nutritional facts.

The same motivation that blew you up
can also bring you down,
You must start with hope, maintain your faith,
and want to turn around.

Your body is a temple,
in which the Holy Spirit dwells,
The perils of obesity
is what causes it to swell.

Obesity is a form of violence
that destroys the temple's walls,
It does not discriminate and traps
all who yield its call.

After God made man and the woman
He took from Adam's rib,
He then made food from the earth
for nutrition on which to live.

So if you are unhappy and overweight,
and harbor inner hate,
Remember all good things are possible
and it's because of what you ate.

To reduce your excess weight
you can start with this positive thought,
God made you in His image
and with Him you can walk.

Change your way of thinking
to be transformed each day,
Apply knowledge, strength and wisdom
to be healthy in His Way.

Begin to eat for life
and not just what taste good,
Eat to nourish your body,
this you really should.

Honor you body,
your spirit too,
And know that God
always loves you.

Obesity is not His intent,
to live more abundantly
is not being over spent.

Eat to live and not to die
must become your new battle cry,
Obesity can become a thing of the past
if you give it a spirit filled try.

After hearing all this, you still find
it hard to lose your excess weight,
Think about those who love you
so much and pray for your sake.

Eliminate all things in your life
that have nothing to do with godly living,
Fall down on your knees, praise His Holy Name
with joy and thanksgiving.

When you look in the mirror
and see a transformed body, and know it was not a diet,
It was the power of God, and faith in His word
that even made you try it.

We wish you good health and life
everlasting in the temple for which you were meant,
Only then will having read this long poem
be blessed time well spent.

Obesity is a killer, but life is forever,
if the choices you make are divine,
The way the Lord lives in His Holy Temple
is the way that I should live in mine.

**Religion should honor God
and do what is good toward humanity.**

*Religion that God our Father
accepts as pure and faultless is this:
to look after orphans and widows
in their distress and to keep oneself
from being polluted by the world.*

James 1:27

Religion

Religion is a complex subject
which is often misunderstood.
It might be practiced in a church,
synagogue, cathedral or mosque
in your neighborhood.

Religion should stand for peace
and faith with a focus on the love of God,
But in some places like the Middle East,
religion involves jihad.

Sectarian groups across the globe
work hard to make known their druthers,
However, it is not our job to sit in judgment
of the religious preference of others.

Religion seems to segregate more people
than it brings together,
Denominations, mega churches and
TV evangelists compete with one another.

Some religious practices are contradicted
by elements of hypocrisy,
Leaders say one thing then do another
to promote their own philosophy.

The separation of church and state
is not the doctrine of every nation,
In countries where theocracies exist
church and state are an amalgamation.

Religion in America is highly varied
with multiple connotations,
Some value the way people pray
and the size of their donations.

Religion in America can be practiced
in several different forms,
Having such freedom makes us subject
to the worlds' envy and scorn.

Can you imagine everyone
being of the same religion?
There would be one less reason
for wars and cultural division.

Diversity of religion gives
Americans many choices,
Where they can practice their beliefs
with uninhibited voices.

Christianity is my religion of choice;
it is how I live my life,
I invite anyone who wants it
to simply accept Jesus Christ.

The way to the Father is through the Son,
according to the word,
This is the choice of the Christian believer
when God's word has been heard.

Religion is more complicated as the
world in which we live gets smaller,
With faith in God and the spirit of Christ
all People will stand taller.

Religion is a fact of life for peoples
of the world, regardless which one they favor,
So choose your religion with the love of God
and the same love for your neighbor.

FAITH

**Keeping God first in your life
will yield many blessings and rewards.**

*Know therefore that the LORD your God is God;
he is the faithful God, keeping his covenant of love
to a thousand generations of those who love him
and keep his commands.*

Deuteronomy 7:9

Remember Me

Remember me and the things I do;
those are the things that will last,
Don't rely on what others do
because those are the things that will pass.

Look to the sky and call upon my name
when life becomes too much,
I will hear your prayer and respond in-kind
with a loving and tender touch.

Remember me when all is well
and blessings are coming your way,
This is not an aberration or stroke of luck
for my love is every day.

In your inner most thoughts my spirit resides
to give you piece of mind,
Your outer being will want to emulate
acts that are divine.

Remember me in all your ways
and walk the straight and narrow,
For I am the one who sees all you do,
my eye is on the sparrow.

Life is short and full of choices
both good to bad,
Live your life in a manner in which
you don't have to wish you had.

Remembering me once you know me
will be required for your judgment,
I am your Lord and savior, who died so
that your life could be more abundant.

So in the final analysis
if remembering me will definitely be your choice,
You will know that you have acted wisely
when in heaven you hear my voice.

BELIEVE

**All sin is harmful to the Spirit
and breaks the laws of God.**

*For the wages of sin is death,
but the gift of God is eternal life
in Christ Jesus our Lord.*

Romans 6:23

Sin; Thought,
Word and Deed

The wages of sin result in death
according to the book of James,
Avoiding sin at any cost
should be a believer's aim.

Yet many people deal with sin
as though it were a game,
They commit a sin, pray for forgiveness
and sin all over again.

This poem is about the silent sin
the one we do by thought,
This type of sin is very deadly
because we believe we can't get caught.

Sin by thought lingers in your mind
and forms a visualization,
You burn with passion and desire
before its full manifestation.

You fantasize about such things
that you do not want to talk,
You are satisfied with this sin
as long as it's just a thought.

When festering in your mind,
thought sin can ruin your spirit life,
It creates frustration, misguided passion,
agony and strife.

What is in your thoughts at some point
will be said and probably done,
So avoid thought sin and its destructive force
before it is begun.

Thought sin is the silent killer
that we place upon our heart,
Even though we know full well
it's tearing us apart.

Thought sin is not spoken, acted out,
but in your mind it will keep,
Even in your thoughts, the things you sow
you will also reap.

Control your thought sin with
the awesome power of God's holy word,
Your inner thoughts will function differently
once the word is heard.

If all else fails convert thought sin
to prayer and focus on your prize,
Sin thought will die, your mind will clear
and your spirit will come alive.

Dear Heavenly Father forgive
our sins of thought, word and deed,
We know that you can read our minds
and know our every need.

We thank you Lord for hearing our prayer
and straightening up our walk,
We thank you God for helping us
to overcome the silent sin of thought.

SIN

**Thankfulness for the goodness of God
should be an ongoing practice.**

*Give thanks in all circumstances,
for this is God's will for you in Jesus Christ.*

1 Thessalonians 5:18

Thanksgiving

Giving thanks to God for all we have
should be a willing and natural reaction,
Yet we take for granted our many blessings
as though we made them happen.

Thanksgiving is celebrated once a year
with a festive family meal,
Thanking God every day for our blessings
would be more like keeping it real.

Thanksgiving is a time to remember the sins,
for which you are forgiven,
Giving thanks for repentance, redemption
and the will to be God driven.

Thanksgiving is a time to pay homage
to those who fight for our nation,
It is one special time among many to express
our sincere appreciation.

Thanksgiving is a time for sharing
with those who may not have as much,
Thanksgiving is a time for humility and caring
with a tender and loving touch.

Thanksgiving is a time to share the bounties
of our cups that have run over,
Especially with endearing people in our lives
who are blessed to be much older.

At Thanksgiving we share family stories
of today's events and those a long time ago,
We reminisce about such oral history
so that our young ones will always know.

New births, graduation, weddings and funerals
are the things that families remember,
These things will occur in the families assembled,
between December and November.

Thanksgiving is a time to see the busy people
we miss because time flies,
It is a joyous time to reconnect
and strengthen loose family ties.

Thanksgiving comes in a beautiful season,
it happens in the fall,
About the time Ohio State and Michigan meet
in a game of football.

There are many joys of Thanksgiving
that we will forever cherish,
With God as the recipient of our thanks,
our spirits will never parish,

Express thanks to God for all your blessings
and live an abundant life,
Give thanks for your parents, children
and your husband or your wife.

Thanksgiving comes on the last
Thursday of November as an official holiday,
But the righteous person who has come to know
Jesus will thank God anyway.

Be obedient to the word of God
and to the things that he would have you do,
And the ultimate blessing that you will receive
is the day that Jesus thanks you.

THANKFUL

**The believer will find joy when
the spirit departs the body and ascends.**

*I tell you the truth, if anyone keeps
my word he will never see death.*

John 8:51

The Passing

When our loved ones forever go away
it seems to be a very solemn day,
With their passing keep in mind,
they were chosen and you were left behind.

We do not know the hour,
the month or even the day,
All we know for certain is
that on earth we cannot stay.

If on the day of their departure
they have accepted the gift of salvation,
There is absolutely no mystery
about their eventual destination.

They do have choices about their fate
while they are yet alive,
Even though life ends in death
from which no one can hide.

The passing can bring about stress,
anxiety and a time in which one grieves,
The grief period can be long or short
depending on what one believes.

The passing is a natural happening;
it is a daily occurrence,
Just be certain that before you pass,
you have acquired a blessed assurance.

Jesus loves criminals too.

But if a wicked man turns away from
all the sins he has committed
and keeps all my decrees
and does what is just and right,
he will surely live; he will not die.

Ezekiel 18:21

Thug Life

Jesus loves thugs too, He just doesn't like what they do.

Lust, stealing and killing violates God's law,
Sin like this makes you live in the raw,

Jesus loves thugs too, He just doesn't like what they do.

Living in sin is a choice that you make,
You can repent and be redeemed for God's sake.

Life is a promise for all who have breath,
But for those who disbelieve it always means death,
For you see, God gives us power to choose between the two.

Jesus loves thugs too, He just doesn't like what they do.

So when you get tired of jails and having no job,
Just remember the alternative is to work and not to rob.
Your circumstances can change under the power of God,
Life has a greater meaning when Jesus is alive within you,

Jesus loves thugs too, He just doesn't like what they do.

A thug hung by Jesus as he died on the cross,
And because Jesus heard his heart, his sole was not lost.
It's never too late for thugs to get straight,
God is patient to claim a believer and will always wait,

Jesus loves thugs too, He just doesn't like what they do.

So take that first step toward a life of salvation,
Let the Bible be your weapon and sever your ties with Satan.

He would much rather have you saved and brand new,
Jesus loves thugs too, He just doesn't like what they do.

To God we pray, so you'll have life in Jesus some day.